CRUEL FEVER OF THE SKY

Carey Scott Wilkerson

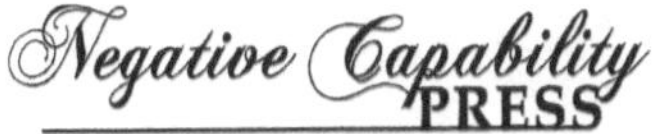
Negative Capability
PRESS

Library of Congress Control Number: 2021937681

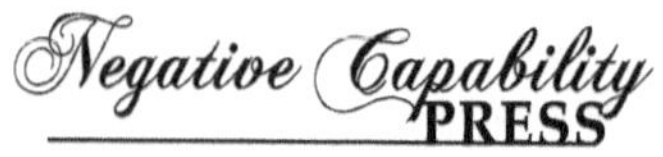

Published by Negative Capability Press
150 Du Rhu Drive, #2202
Mobile, AL 36608
www.negativecapabilitypress.org

Cover: Photo by Jaanus Jagomägi on Unsplash

For my family.

Acknowledgments

I wish to thank the following friends and colleagues for their insights into early versions of these poems and for their kind support of my work: David Bottoms, Marian Carcache, Judith Carson, Joel Chace, Simona Chitescu-Weik, Nancy Correro, Caroline Crew, Jim and Candace Davenport, Greg Emilio, Stephen Foster, Mac Gay, Allen Gee, Gail Greenblatt, John Holman, Susan Hrach, Melissa Dickson Jackson, Mostafa Jalal, Anna King, Jessica Lindberg, Judi Livingston, Josh Martin, Gregg Murray, Andi Rogers Patton, Mamie Willoughby Pound, the Quinton Family (Angel, Will, BB), Aaron Sanders, Ann Sandy-Elrod, Mike Saye, Marissa Stockton, Leon Stokesbury, Paige Sullivan, and Natalia Temesgen. Special thanks to Beth Gylys, Tara McGhee, Nick Norwood, Sue Walker, and William Walsh. My thanks, as well, to the editors of the publications and other media in which many of these poems first appeared, sometimes in a different form.

"Gated Communities" was a 2016 Pushcart Prize nominee

"Toolkit" also appeared as "Toolkit for Felix" in *Ars Minotaurica* (New Plains Press, 2012)

"Descending Order" was chosen by *The MacGuffin* to be among its representative Sestinas for the Formal Poetry Fall 2020 issue, Vol 36.3

Birmingham Arts Journal: "Toolkit"

Bright Illuminations: The Art of Margie Bright Ragland and the Words of Others: "Ceci n'est pas un Oiseau"

E•ratio: "Dear Ariadne"; "Directions for Following Your Irrational Heart During the Navigation of a "Tempestina"

The HitchLit Review: "Fairy Godmother's Lament"; "Ornithology"; "Scientific Method"

The James Dickey Review: "Fall on Ocean Avenue"; "Mediterraneo"; "Summer's End"; "William Penn Omni"

KSKQ News and Interviews: "Crystal Blue Persuasion"; "Mirroir Noir"; "Prendre des Vacances"

The MacGuffin Journal: "Descending Order"

Muse/A: "Chattahoochee Epistemology"; "Gated Communities"; "Los Feliz"

McRitchie-Hollis Museum Exhibition Chapbook—Hats, Caps, Bonnets, and Fedoras: "Family Trees"

Negative Capability: "Dinner Blessing"; "Nocturne for the Old Style"

Newnan-Coweta Magazine: "The Acceleration of Gravity"

Night's Magician: Poems About the Moon: "Astronomy Lesson"

Otoliths: "A Life in Art"; Saving a Marriage"; "Two Photographs"

Sanctuary: "Anna Moffo's *Traviata*"; "Career Trajectory"; "The Sunset Götterdämmerung,"

Stone, River, Sky: An Anthology of Georgia Poems: "This is Only a Test"

The Zoomoozophone Review: "Parabolic Curve for Icarus"

Contents

Descending Order

Icarus, free-falling out of the sky,
wonders whether he should finally speak
the embarrassing truth about losing—
how its dark entanglement of desire
with the complicated need to forget—
eventually melts down in plain old failure

That his own project is framed by failure
feels like some cruel fever of the sky
in which the poor afflicted birds forget
to flap their wings. Even the emus speak
guardedly about a secret desire
to have prophetic visions while losing

altitude over the sea, how losing
one's life is somehow a failure
of the imagination. Still, desire
is how Icarus understands the sky,
with all those ups and downs, so to speak.
Daedalus, his father, said, "Don't forget

the sun," but off the record said, "forget
about winning and think more of losing
with some panache. And, incidentally, speak
of disaster as *triumph in failure*."
For Icarus, the problem of the sky
begins and ends with his view of desire

as a kind of death wish, which means desire
can cause even sincere fools to forget
real differences between earth and sky.
This is perhaps the charm of a losing
proposition; it's the sound of failure
ricocheting through every word we speak.

So, here he is, trying at last to speak
plainly without betraying his desire
for fame as a celebrated failure:
"High-flying winners will forget
that the secret to a life of losing
is a fear of heights and a love of sky."

Let Icarus dream his dreams and forget
whether losing ends as failure.
Desire is always falling from the sky.

Part One

The Sunset Götterdämmerung

...the expensive delicate ship that must have seen
Something amazing, a boy falling out of the sky,
Had somewhere to get to and sailed calmly on

—W.H. Auden, "Musée des Beaux Arts"

Los Feliz

Because there are no fireflies in Los Angeles
we strung faerie lights through pepper trees
that summer beside the cedar-wood bungalow
in our narrow canyon. The Rossini 78s we found
at some Saturday-morning bazaar threaded
von Stade's *Cenerentola* through the drone of traffic
tangled in palms on Franklin Avenue, just below.
Sheila, the neighbor, claimed the power of crystals
could save us from conspiracies, government smog,
and urban dreams with disappointing endings.
Her boyfriend, Bernard, a contract pilot for the police
promised to bless our love from the helicopter's cockpit
during a pre-dawn flyover at four-thousand feet.
You cooked up a pan of eggplant parm for the actresses
living in the Sixth Street loft when they all agreed
both to be in my play *and* not take their clothes off onstage.
In the farmer's market dumpster, I found new brushes
tied with yarn to unopened jars of shimmering gesso.
And I stretched canvas for the triptych you were painting
every night downstairs while I only pretended to sleep
but instead lay wondering what secret name for
fate I could invoke to keep you from leaving. I wish
I'd asked — even just once — if you knew the stars
in Andromeda are visible from the top
of the Ferris wheel on the Santa Monica Pier.

Crystal Blue Persuasion

It started with a polished amethyst in the aloe plant
on the window-sill above the kitchen sink, we think.
Next must have been the pale shard of blue topaz
wedged under the stack of old *New Yorker* magazines.
We had canceled the subscription but couldn't bear
to throw them away and needed the cartoons
in a difficult year — so difficult that in an unguarded
moment, I tried to eat three caramel moonstones I found
behind our signed photograph of Montserrat Caballé,
believing them to be unwrapped marzipan pralines
from Canter's Deli. In the entire Los Angeles basin,
could I have been the only fool trying to eat rocks?

Wednesday night, cherry carnelian under a sofa cushion.
Thursday night, a strand of beaded quartz under our bed
Upstairs. We did not mind living quirky lives,
but agreed this was more quirk than we required.
Friday morning at DuPar's Diner, the crazy neighbors
Sheila and Bernard asked if we had noticed the obvious
good effects of the emergency exorcism Sheila had performed
on our house last weekend while we were away
and whether we felt the endorphin swell of healing crystal loves?

That's how they said it: *loves* in the plural, as though
everyone knew *loves* were formed over eons in the furnace
of the planet. We were ready to draw the line at Sheila's wild act
of breaking and entering when Rhoda Barkhado — the Somali
pastry chef, whose sour cream waffles and umber maple syrup
had hypnotized the city — arrived at our table in a turquoise sarong
wondering aloud *Who would dare ask for a day better than this?*

Prendre des Vacances

If we took a holiday yeah
Took some time to celebrate
Just one day out of life
It would be
It would be so nice.

—Madonna

That summer we acquired our first fire-sale book collection:
for only ten dollars, eight paper sacs from *Rock 'n' Roll Ralph's,*
which we discovered contained one-hundred twelve titles,
all but nine of them, *en* (let's not blame each other today) *Français.*
In a smear of afternoon sun on the wrought-iron
chaise longue, you were eating pepper-fried plantains,
weeping for Emma Bovary, asking if I envied the way
people in 19th-century novels are always traveling to Rouen
for a weekend or Lucerne for the season? And I answered,
having no money, we might simply fake a vacation
to Catalina Island—or as it would be an illusion anyway—
perhaps to Provence. Because I was unsure of the translation,
I tried it a couple of different ways: *faire des vacances fictifs?*
avoir des faux vacances? Not only was I getting nowhere,
I was lost in Sartre's *Huis Clos,* silently urging his trapped characters
to talk like real people, to think of the mysterious door
as an escape from clichéd despair. Just before sunset, our neighbors,
Sheila and Bernard—native SoCal spiritualists, whom we found
unbound by time and space—lowered a needle onto vinyl
and pushed from their Peavey amp a single chorus of Madonna's *Holiday*
through a tangle of mariposa lilies separating their lot from ours.

Watts Towers

Bite your lip and take a trip
Though there may be wet road ahead
And you cannot slip so what you wanna do
Just move on up for peace you will find
Into the steeple of beautiful people where there's only one kind

    —Curtis Mayfield, *Move On Up*

Look at us, three hours now, maundering
with your skeptical UCLA undergraduates
among Sabata Rodia's curated dreamscapes.
We're theorizing in this bone-lattice found-object
world rendered in plaster, mesh, ceramic, rebar.
We're talking erasure and context, peering into
vanity mirrors split in some minor, forgotten quake—
green glass of 7-Up bottles, rail-yard scrap metal
from the Pacific-Electric Wilmington line, touching
seashells big as palm fronds, opalescent and lurid:
an accretion of other men's daily anarchies fixed
in twilit ceremony, drizzled with homemade concrete.
Your most promising student asks: *But is it art?*
Your lips don't move, but I hear someone whisper
there are no perfect solutions, even in this place
where *Nuestro Pueblo,* our town—like the rockets
of naïve 1950s science fiction, with fins, portals,
and one fearless pilot—points its spires straight up.

Fairy Godmother's Lament

I shouldn't talk about clients this way,
but Djamila the Tunisian seamstress,
who asked for an infinite supply of fabrics,
was found suffocated in her garden
of wild cinnamon trees under
six tons of lavender charmeuse.

Meredith, an up-market estate planner
in Pacific Palisades wanted her newborn twins
in the best possible college, at which instant
Kirabelle and Mathilde vanished from the nursery
and materialized in Professor Celeste Rosen's
Women's Studies seminar at Bryn Mawr. The mother
was charged with endangerment and the babies dropped
from class for failure to pay the tuition and ancillary fees.

Alexander wanted only money and so, lost his
possessions—everything in his house, including his wife,
having turned into stacks of unmarked, non-sequential
hundred-dollars bills. Phyllis wanted only to be in love
and so, lost all her friends, who could not love her
in the same way and who could not bear her
long life of betrayed silence.
I just never learned to say "no."

If I had one wish, it would not be for the end
of desire's secret madness or even for a planet
of rational, compassionate hearts. Instead,
I would ask for some place where magic
is just words and the wand, a piece of pine.

The Acceleration of Gravity

for Mayhaley Lancaster of Coweta County
(1875-1955: feminist, unlicensed attorney,
fortune teller, and wise mind whom many
thought to be a witch.)

It's not later than supper when,
as from a tale no one quite believes,
Mayhaley Lancaster—seamstress, notary,
and the county's own witch—
looks up to see Icarus splash
into the Chattahoochee River.

She rows out to meet him in a boat,
stitched together from pine splinters
and biscuit dough: it's a conversation piece
to be sure, though strictly speaking mostly
a matter of timing as she has just set the table.
Of course, this has happened before
and is an open secret around here:
Leonardo in his proto-helicopter, the Wright Brothers,
and Santa Claus, all arrived in the same way—
wet and confused but, like Icarus, coherent enough to eat.

She pours sweet tea and salts some tomatoes.
He complains about mythology
and being trapped inside a narrative,
lost in the bog of legend.
She fills his plate with butter beans
and cornbread fried on the stove.
Icarus laments the contradictory relationship
between history and memory.

Mayhaley discovers some of last year's
hot-pepper jelly in the back of the pantry.
He apologizes for talking so far above her head.
She forgives him for being neurotic and aloof.
Mayhaley repairs his wax wings with a quilting knot
she learned in town. Icarus signs her guestbook
both in English and in Greek. They shake hands
under the April sky in a crescent of Georgia light,
and in a flourish, he flies back into his story.

She observes this from the middle of the Chattahoochee
in a boat she stitched together from bee wings,
Paraffin wax, and the names of her favorite clouds.

A Life in Art

Then they set their bloody hands on Orpheus, and gathered, like birds that spy the owl, the bird of night, wandering in the daylight, or as in the amphitheatre, on the morning of the staged events, on either side, a doomed stag, in the arena, is prey to the hounds.

—Ovid, *The Metamorphoses, Book XI*

The Maenads, tweaking in their paranoid
ecstasies, decided they had no other choice
but to pound on Orpheus's stately front door,
shrieking their intent to dismember him.
Lost in silent despair over a failed attempt
at rescuing his wife Eurydice from Hell,
he forgot his manners and failed again:
forgetting, this time, to invite his own dread
murderers in for cocktails, which they drank
anyway when it was all over. Some believed
Orpheus died when they ripped his limbs
from his torso. Others felt he had been crushed
when they burst into the foyer and a decorative
chandelier plunged into his face, still torqued
by love's naïve and deferent smile. Scattering
his body parts along the freeway, in rest-stop
bathrooms and abandoned construction sites,
the Maenads rendered the night down to a stub
of quiet shame, pulled over at last, praying
for sleep enough to leave behind death's wet smile.
And from the trunk of their stolen Caddy,
the head of Orpheus sang for them a muffled lullaby.

Fall on Ocean Avenue

I saw Sisyphus in agonizing torment trying to roll a huge stone to the top of a hill. He would brace himself, and push it towards the summit with both hands, but just as he was about to heave it over the crest its weight overcame him, and then down again to the plain came bounding that pitiless boulder.

—Homer, *The Odyssey, Book XI*

October night on the Santa Monica Pier, atop the giant Ferris wheel,
its glow spilled down the beach and stretched across the bay,

a funhouse parody of ourselves on uncertain waves, churning, cold
in the carnival moon. Neither of us believed this ritual could save us,

but we'd tried it anyway all summer. We held on tight, felt once again
the lift of our foolish schemes, the miracle of your mother's gardenias,

transplanted in the wrong season but trilling the air with white perfume
between the tool shed and the pepper tree, our reckless thrill in squandering

half the grocery money on a print of Titian's Sisyphus from the MOCA
souvenir store. Maybe we sensed that we owed Sisyphus and your mother

a final push at the impossible. As a merciful operator paused us at the apex,
we strained like teenagers over the dizzy edge, memorizing the still life

of our finished turn—a neon sunflower hovering on the ocean—until,
as we knew they would, levers moved, time ran out, and gravity let us down.

*MOCA is the Museum of Contemporary Art, Los Angeles

Bela Lugosi Meets a Brooklyn Gorilla, 1952

Dracula: To die, to be really dead, that must be glorious!
Mina: Why, Count Dracula!
Dracula: There are far worse things awaiting man than death.

—Dracula, Universal Studios, 1931

On the screen, I can see you don't understand what's happening,
what has happened. You're afraid to ask how a gratuitous close-up

finds you suddenly old, a mad scientist now, draped in a lab coat,
narrating straight into the camera a plot to steal the leading man's girl

and then turn him into a dancing gorilla. Half-forgotten and broke,
you seem happy, a grateful clown, hired by telegram to play Dr. Zabor,

third banana to B-list Martin and Lewis knockoffs feeding themselves
on your addiction to heroin, on the derelict kitsch of your morphine cure,

on your dead fame. After the wrap party, you'll be alone on a plywood set,
and, later, stalk the supper clubs of east Wilshire, trying to score,

maybe just enough to fill one syringe, dim your blood from Technicolor
to black and white. Just know I'm praying that the projectionist

will wind back the last reel, free you from irony and Rock 'n' Roll, restore you
to the crypt and moon terror, a surrender of veins in the ingénue's throat.

Dinner Blessing

After Goya's Saturn Devouring His Son, 1819-1823

Cronus explains to his wife that eating
their children is proof of his love for her,
no less than the fat lavender candles,
hyacinth soaps, and long-stem red roses
he brings home on their anniversary.
He's quick to remind her that she's had
no cause lately to worry about what's for supper
or apologize for the same old dish.

And it's true, Rhea is a pushover
for most of her husband's romantic stunts,
but suspects that three devoured offspring
in a row proves they've simply stopped trying
to surprise each other, that they've just fallen
into the cliché of worn-out routine
and numbing repetition that consumes
so many happy marriages these days.

She's thinking of saving her next born: Zeus,
whom she hopes will someday cut his father
wide open, freeing his siblings inside;
and then maybe — before the blame,
the guilt, and of course the war —
they'll sit for once, like all good families,
together at the dining room table.

Career Trajectory

Christmas 1932, highfalutin members
of the New York Opera Guild reported
seeing Icarus plummet into the Hudson River,
and later, napping on the Staten Island Ferry.

It is believed that in July of 1945,
Icarus plunged straight into the shockwave
of the first Atomic Bomb test at Alamogordo, New Mexico,
but, true to form, was later photographed
at an after-party on the shore of Lake Bonita
standing next to Oppenheimer himself.

Norman Mailer, while covering a mass-exorcism
and failed levitation of the Pentagon in 1967
may or may not have observed himself observing
Icarus arcing over the Washington Monument
and into the Potomac.

Early Shuttle astronauts whisper stories
of a "winged anomaly over North Africa."
As late as the mid-90's Jacques Cousteau's pastry chef
noted in his log *"quelque chose étrange"*
over the Great Barrier Reef.
And even today, surfers consider it a given
that if Icarus buzzes Huntington Beach,
their prayers will be measured in miracle waves.

But Icarus has grown weary
of the spectacle of his own life.
The looping cycle of cataclysm,
flying at the sun, falling into the sea
seems less a mythic ritual
and more an addiction to his own ruin.
He knows he's pandering and a certain
ambivalence is beginning to show.

On the other hand, he speaks often
of retirement, of simply taking off
and never coming back.
To be sure, it is not altogether clear
what his departure would mean —
the end of his myth?
the end of all myths related to his myth?
the end of myth itself?
And though he concedes these scenarios
are disruptive, incoherent, perhaps
not finally possible, he dreams nonetheless
in the language of escape.

Still, life is hard.
Everyone has a job to do.
So, here he is, doomed again
pushing up into the vast blue canvas of fate,
imagining that moment when he either
descends in tragic splendor
or dares an inconceivable shattering
of narrative logic and some other
way toward knowing.

This tension, however, is not discernible
from far below where his tiny reflection,
warped in comic refraction,
passes just now across bubbles
in a jar of local honey.

Mirroir Noir

From the Griffith Park Observatory, we cannot fail
to see the jump-cut playback of years spent

tracking the suspects through our double-crossed
streets, under the slow pulse

of Old Hollywood. We always knew
where to find them and what scam they were running.

Today for instance, one of them tries
a harmless lie about hours of traffic on the 405,

more believable, he supposes, than the truth of his wandering
all day through the Central Library looking

for the right words. And yesterday, the other swears, was nothing
more than a lingering lunch with her friend

from Malibu. Their stories, while plausible, don't finally add up,
and it's only a matter of time before they implicate

each other. Because we feel one or both might be planning
an escape, we're looking at their movements,

hoping for a clue. We spot them canning habañero sweet pickles
but lose them when they stop eating together.

We catch them laughing on the Third Street Promenade
but hear only silence in their bedroom.

They're onto us. We've been made. From the observatory
colonnade, the city sweeps out before us

in a densely-plotted weave of light and shadow,
no leading cast, no clear resolution,

only a hazy view of Melrose
where the Cosmopolitan Book Shop used to be.

Saving a Marriage

My wife is the cause of my journey.

—Orpheus upon entering the Underworld to retrieve Eurydice
—Ovid, *The Metamorphoses, Book X*

Orpheus perceives the scale of trouble
he's inviting into his absurd life:
a desperate mission to rescue, from death
itself, a woman he knows he could love
forever, who has inspired his music,
and who waits now in terminal silence.

Strictly speaking, he's not against silence
and, indeed, freely admits the trouble
began with his compulsion for music.
Not to mention, he has heard all his life
that women are moved by the arts and love
musicians, which certainly means the death

of virtue and, in this case, just plain death.
Orpheus feels he should at least silence
those critics who glibly claim that his love
for Eurydice caused her more trouble
than he's worth and that she paid with her life
while he prattles on about his music.

But she is the source of that same music.
And even if he has to perform Death
Metal, it will be the show of his life,
power chords shredding darkness and silence.
If the Underworld really wants trouble,
he will bring some down in the name of love,

even as he wonders whether that love
will be enough for her, if his music
has the power to calm fear and trouble
in the heart of any who has seen death
up close or wandered so long in silence.
He can save her but never know her life

or what it means to live inside a life
transformed by the crisis of a man's love.
For Eurydice, the days are silence;
for Orpheus, they are only music.
He will never understand her, or death.
Or the way he needs this world of trouble.

But for now, the silence and the trouble
in his life mean less to him than music.
And his best love song will be sung to death.

The Sunset Götterdämmerung

Götterdämmerung translates to "Twilight of the Gods"
and is the last opera in Richard Wagner's *Ring Cycle*

We always took the surface streets
from our house in Nichols Canyon, east
through low notes on the long sine wave
of downtown traffic where we endured
our seasonal Wagner in that outré L.A. idiom:
Das Rheingold set in a surreal theme park, grim
Siegfried re-imagined in a nightmare zoo,
the dragon a sympathetic captive in some prison
of urban trauma. We probably felt the same,
watching *Die Valküre* stripped to industrial-chic
minimalism at the Hollywood Bowl with $11 popcorn
and projections of the helicopters from *Apocalypse Now*.

They never did stage a complete Ring until years later,
our subscription expired and, you, back in Atlanta.
The papers said that this tragic last opera — the one
we never saw together — played just the way we
suspected it might: to big crowds and mixed reviews.
But ours — the one we dreamed about on that last trip
to Santa Barbara — had flying saucers hovering
on the west end of Sunset, taking one last look at our city
where it reaches the Pacific Coast Highway, and is gone.

Part Two

Chattahoochee Epistemology

There are moments a man turns from us
Whom we have all known until now…

—James Dickey, "Drowning with Others"

City Girl in Half Light

Remind me please how the whole affair
Left you somehow with only spilled coordinates
Yet flawless timing for a wounded stare
When I stumbled on those flâneur degenerates—
Whom you called close friends—splicing the train
Schedule into our numbered Titian print again,
To say nothing of how I wanted mostly to kiss
You more but learned by long division to do with less
Certainty in all things. I'm half hoping you've met
My *Doppelgänger* and have fallen secretly in city love,
Leaving me lost in my double remove
Waiting for you in half-night on a city street
Where trouble is both wave and particle,
The moon, a kind of miracle.

Chattahoochee Epistemology

The Oracle of Podunk says that we are, all of us, ordained priests
of the next ten minutes of our lives. From his camp, a ruin, cold

on the backwater in Bull Slough, he comes—wearing his John Deere hat—
to meet the penitent, requiring at his Friday dispensation of grace,

hot pepper jelly for his butter beans, and Old No.7 for his concentration.
We were stupid from school once and had the gall to ask him why

so many river-bank wise men seem to live under flapping blue tarps
and drink like cliché uncles? And why, if he really could see the future,

didn't he turn out better? His silence, a reply strict as Leviticus,
held us in its undertow until we were men with secrets of our own.

Sunday, after church, chastened by slow years, I drive down one last time
to the river with fried egg sandwiches in tin foil, a thermos of Smirnoff,

and an apology letter I spent two weeks writing. The oracle rows across,
receives my gifts, drifts back to his camp: exactly five minutes each way.

Standing in black mud on the shore, I watch him take communion—
eat a sandwich, sip the vodka, and with my letter, light kindling for his fire.

Dear Ariadne,

I wish that you, Theseus hadn't killed the Minotaur, half man, half bull, wielding a knotted club in your strong hand: and that I hadn't given you the thread that marked your way back, the thread so often received back into the hand that drew it.

—Ovid, *The Heroides, Book X*

I see you counting the minutes on Crete—
your black hair scintillant in September's
curved light—glamorous in perfect boredom.

You already suspect that Theseus
is a fraud and will leave you trapped again
on another island, another shore.

You know you'll never be properly Greek,
see Athens, or wear incarnadine silk
to a hero's bed. You'll never be free.

Still, you have given him his only chance
to survive the Minotaur's labyrinth.
And he's down there, unspooling your thread

behind him, dreaming up a big parade
for the conqueror himself. But you
are holding the other end of that thread

and could choose simply to let go. What then?
For you, betrayal is unthinkable
even if his heart is an endless maze

of broken promises. So, wait for him
as the beach under you sluices away.
Listen close to his fantastical tale

and its version of your future with him.
Pull the steel of his sword against your hip
bone when he holds you, when he declares you

his. Kiss him like the lover you wanted
him to be. And under the folding sky,
let him feel the grit of sand in your mouth.

Ornithology

From this upstairs window, I can only hope
that the White Heron stalking among the blue sage

doesn't notice me — self-conscious and boring —
watching him in the pewter evening light,

searching the shallows for unwary minnows
and snails. We saw him last year, scaring

the sunning turtles off their logs, practicing
his repertoire of stop-motion dances

and now these pirouettes, precise, silent
in Georgia clay. Unlike the glamorous Hollywood

Kestrels we saw swooping over the Silver Lake
reservoir, we have not learned patience enough

to wait for a changing season; you've migrated
too soon back to Los Angeles and I keep forgetting

to call. Still, here, Purple Martins are hunting mosquitoes,
and our Heron is nesting in the impossible space

between us under a sky gone suddenly dark
with rumors of September, except for the last

stray filaments of the Perseid, darting ghosts
of fireflies, barely visible in the mirror of the pond.

Mediterraneo

My father is riding a bike in Barcelona
through Gaudi's Park Carmel, under warping
rooflines of modernist chic. With him is a woman
whose name my mother never cared to know,
a black-haired Catalonian orchid, balancing
on the handlebars. Her head is tossed back
in laughter and her tiny left hand is on my father's
handkerchief—tied in the perfect square knot
of Service Dress Blues—pulling him toward her,
into the center of the frame. Fifteen years later,
he teaches me to tie that same knot in both
Navy and civilian styles. I ask him about the girl
in the fading Kodamatic picture in a photo album
labeled *Enlisted Years*. He remembers only two details:
that her name was Antonella, which means flower;
and that in his letter to my mother in Alabama—written
the next day from his bunk on the U.S.S. Roosevelt—
he noted how from the deck of the ship passing through
the Straits of Gibraltar, he could see the coasts of Europe
to starboard, North Africa to port, and that he longed for
the beaches of Gulf Shores, the harbor of Mobile Bay.

Summer's End

We were boys somewhere between Star Wars
and the swarm of girls on purple bicycles
buzzing in driveways and knowing far more
than us about the world — these oracles
of the neighborhood, who had begun in spring
a coordinated campaign of whispering
sundresses and secret plotlines, quoting
made-up love songs and explaining nothing.
John Chancellor warned that Skylab was falling
out of its orbit, so we searched for fiery signs
together, forgot our names and our parents calling
us to our homes among sleeping roses, silent pines.
NASA said the wreckage rained over Australia,
but I swear we saw it blazing over Alabama.

Trees

From my kitchen window, I pretend not to notice a dark shape
at the edge of my vision, beyond the back-yard,
through a stand of pulpwood pine. It's not the same shadow
that stalked my father among the Pignut Hickories
beneath the Halawakee grist mill just before he joined the Navy,
photographed orchids in Barcelona, and came back for my mother.
Nor is it the loping spring gloam that followed my grandfather
onstage under the canopy of Occonee (he pronounced it "oakney") Pecans
the night he called the county dance, played "Tennessee Waltz"
on a borrowed guitar, and met his wife. No, my drifting shade is patient,
cooperative, has me figured out. It knows that come Christmas, I'll marvel
at the family's new children with names so on-trend, the pronunciations
are still in doubt. Surely, there must be a Farmer's Almanac chart
for these generations of perennials coming up like volunteer tomatoes
in Roll-Tide crimson, even War-Eagle orange and blue: signs and wonders
of dynastic games their fathers have willed to them. My cousins are wise,
planting their twilights under ball fields or deep in sensible gardens.
The pretty girls they married watch them as they cut back rows
of Crepe Myrtle, teaching them to grow in the sun.

Anna Moffo's *Traviata*

She watched me watching her watching me—
both of us, still, in the unsettled light
of early spring. But it was late in the day,
and Anna Moffo could certainly wait—
perhaps forever—in her glamorous pose
on the cover of that RCA record.
I could never quite find Verdi in her voice,
but her Violetta left me hurt, awkward;
I made a pirate Traviata on a cassette for the car
I wasn't old enough to drive and, blaring, sped
past the fields where once the county fair
seemed to play all the music I would ever need.
I knew she was tragic, just from the sound
of an aria I never understood until I grew old.

Scientific Method

NOUN: a method of procedure consisting in systematic observation, measurement, experiment, and the formulation, testing, and modification of hypotheses.

Tonight, I have slipped on a banana peel.
In a Kroger parking lot. In the rain. For science,
of course. I confess that I find it hard to believe
myself, but I hear a startled shopper cry out:
"Look at that lunatic slipping on a banana peel!"
This is proof that I have survived the head trauma
of experiments involving bananas, parking lots,
and rain. And the strangeness of night.

Sure, I considered other scenarios: a series of trip wires,
a golf ball out of nowhere, a puddle of butter custard
spread across my path. Or, without warning, my assistant
(unpaid) could simply throw me to the ground.
This discussion ended when I asked if he might enjoy
putting in a little overtime whisking the custard (see above),
and, in a regrettable confusion over nomenclature,
he resigned and called a lawyer. Hence, the banana.

Lovers claim that falling hard bends the world's axis
and I only want to see if what they say is true.
I'd hate to come this far and fail my first test
in slapstick philosophy, but I have no theory of pain.
And yet here I am on my back, squinting at a sky
now spun by the torque of reappearing stars,
thinking that clowns always make this look good
because the body naturally knows how to swoon.

Nocturne for the Old Style

I'll break my staff,
Bury it certain fathoms in the earth,
And deeper than did ever plummet sound
I'll drown my book.

—William Shakespeare, *The Tempest*

Prospero, you know that I found your book
in a doomed schooner under Mobile Bay
and, in January's failing light, read
your history of how things disappear,
its pages fragile as an errant ghost
believing itself somehow home again,
wandering freely among the living:
a naïve clown lost in his stupid dream.

Still, I will not concede the death of art
or claim to understand how you left it
without much explanation or regret
in your rounded sleep. Let me stay awake
while there is yet hope for resurrection
and healing words at the end of the line.

Gated Community

Once upon a time there was an old mother pig who had three little pigs and not
enough food to feed them. So when they were old enough, she sent them out into the
world to seek their fortunes.

—*English Fairy Tales*, retold by Flora Annie Steel, 1922

The three little pigs are at home tonight
in a newly reinforced townhouse, safe

from the world's dangers. They are surrounded
by smart and friendly people of good will

whose polite, bilingual children all love
the pigs' quiet grace and uncluttered style.

They have even attended barbeques
by self-cleaning salt-water pools. Why not?

Life is good in an exclusive address;
there are no big problems, and no bad news.

Yet, when the head of the Neighborhood Watch
is reported missing, the sky turns wild,

first heaving, then pulsing with gale-force wind.
News footage shows nice, respectable homes

blown off their foundations, clean parallel
streets spun into knots, blasted to ruin.

The three little pigs, pursued by some old
and exquisite menace find themselves

squealing in carnival terror, grunting
obscenities into thick, sweet mud,

ripping up azaleas, wolfing down slop:
bungling on the patio, defecating on the lawn.

Tomorrow, surveying the damage, they
might well be observed clutching three little

Bibles, fat faces grim with empathy,
their tears of joy disguised by morning rain.

Part Three

Departures

What do they wish from the voyage
But to awaken far away
By miracle free from every harm…

—Donald Justice, "Sestina on Six
Words by Weldon Kees"

Two Photographs

1. Taormina, Sicily

Even such was the descent of that ravine,
And on the border of the broken chasm
The infamy of Crete was stretched along,

Who was conceived in the fictitious cow;
And when he us beheld, he bit himself,
Even as one whom anger racks within.

—Dante, *Inferno, Canto XII*

Behind you, I can see the fountain spill
water over seven-terraced marble pools
beneath a sculpture of the Minotaur
as he appears in six sad lines of Dante,
frightened, alone at the black precipice
of a ravine. And behind the fountain,
with a view of Mt. Etna, Italy's
most active volcano, is our cheap suite
on the ground floor of Hotel Villa Paradiso.

2. Six Minutes after a sandwich
in Dante Park, New York City

We saw her circling the Revson Fountain
one October night in the Plaza at Lincoln Center.
I wanted to know whether she had ever sung
Euridice in Los Angeles. But you, the quick-draw,
had good sense enough to ask her for a selfie.
Yes, I took the picture but with your iPhone
and thus have no record of the sublime
Catherine Malfitano in the moment
just before she crossed the esplanade into the dark.

Leaving Israel

The moment you insisted that we break
the rules by sneaking across the border
into Jordan—entrusting our good lives
to your friends who bumbled all season
up and down the beaches of Tel Aviv—
I knew the Holy City of Petra
would never be quite enough
to keep you happy. I gave our driver my soap stone
chess set while you charmed the Bedouin guards
with what must have been one of your risqué
jokes in the Hebrew-Arabic patois
that saved us from paying dumb-tourist bribes
and got our rent lowered back in L.A.
That night it was your body
that slipped past its given outline, purling
to the hamsa stitch of our blanket,
in a sacred place under a Moon
that snuffed out the monastery candles.

Omni, William Penn

For the ultimate in luxury, our 38 deluxe suites are adorned with the finest touches for the most discriminating traveler. Discover Pittsburgh accommodations that blend the past and present perfectly at Omni William Penn Hotel.

—Omni Publicity, LLC

I suspect it is impossible
to travel anywhere by Greyhound bus—
let's say even from Pittsburgh to Erie—
given what I know about the creases
of pressed metal holding me to the road,
a bloom of humid May turning outside
my window; shameful, how little I've seen,
except by leaving and mostly by night.

An honest man would find a good hotel
and just wait here for *other* cities to arrive,
their dazed citizens searching for Pittsburgh,
where steel mills could restart in an instant,
and where Billy Conn had his own parade
the day after he nearly beat Joe Louis.

Astronomy Lesson

Icarus is a lunar impact crater that lies on the Moon's far side. It has a worn rim and
a relatively wide inner wall. A small crater lies across the southern rim, and the side
bulges outward slightly along the southwestern face. There is a disproportionately tall
central peak located near the crater midpoint.

—Gazeteer of Planetary Nomenclature

Icarus landed on the Moon's dark side
and now believes himself part of a cosmic
charade designed to keep mythic failures
hidden from public scrutiny, ashamed
of their history. Deep in his crater,
he relives versions of his own story:
plunging first into the Aegean Sea,
then diving straight through Victoria Falls,
splashing down in a glass of Chardonnay,
in backyard swimming pools, and in lovers'
last tears. Even as his father's voice warns
him against self-parody, his crater's
center peak pushes at a cloudless sky,
hangs in space, waiting for the sun to rise.

Directions for Following
Your Irrational Heart
During the Navigation of a Tempestina

Forget almost everything you believe
about the nature of the given world
and instead imagine here a blank page,
an inscrutable and silent machine
for dreaming, for documenting the names
of everyone looking up at the sky.

Because we can, let's say that this same sky
is dense with winged poets — who all believe
in truth — pointing their fingers, naming names,
swooping in wild gyres and plotting a world
where parts of speech turn inside the machine
of desire and love spins out from the page.

Words, then, are no more phantoms of the page
than stars a cruel trick of the night sky.
We've noticed too that love is a machine
with many missing parts, lost, we believe
somewhere off the right margin of the world
on an island of exiles with French names.

Back at the writing desk, our notebook names
all winged poets' flight times on the first page,
every one departing for the same world.
Their stylized ambivalence crowds the sky.
On the final page, you better believe
there is a sketch for some flying machine,

made, surely, for those who need a machine
for reversals, slow erasure of names,
or anything a poet might believe
herself to have conjured from a lost page
that fell from an alphabetical sky,
tattered left margins of another world.

Yet, it's clear that any world is our world,
that life has been good in our own machine,
warm under a clear canonical sky,
with our boring books, reciting the names
of poets who died far above the page
showing doomed Icarus how fools believe.

So, the given world is held in the names
of secret machines hardwired to the page:
hard to believe, but then again: It's the sky!

Parabolic Curve for Icarus

I

As a rule, Icarus prefers the fast freedom
of a vertical drop
to that vertiginous arc in gravity's slow thrall.

These days, of course, a doomed aesthete
plying the ionosphere
has lost some of its early provocation.

Spectacle reads as lurid propaganda
plunging through clouds
dotting lines over maps of warm water.

He would not deny a certain delight
in surrendering the myth
falling out of canonical favor.

And whatever remains of that reckless enterprise —
perilous, irreal — is folded into worn wings,
rubbed and hurting in the plain light of day.

II

From this height, the lights in the railyard
oscillate in early spring's pale skein, mapping

the migration of indeterminate troubles
across colonnades in the city below.

Veiled by the shadow of some cathedral spire,
chess and lunacy converge in the park, as from

remote frontiers of privilege and squalor
clowns and ghosts trundle, ambivalent under the sun.

Here, then, is a world swooping up to meet
the falling feet of one who plummets forever,

who may yet splash down in The Aegean or Brussels
or at Black Mountain College, but who by his nature

dreams only of points fixed in space,
Newtonian tyrannies descending through

symmetrical calamities of the Western heart,
winged, incongruent, lost.

Toolkit

For this experiment, you will need:
projections of other places
disciplines of irony
you will need the Doppler effect
a line-item wrecking crew
one of these, or two
or, three and your dignity
a well-made chair
a taxonomy of beetles
the undeserved trust of scholars
notes scribbled on a peeled apple
or a pair
of apples
you will need declarations of love
lapses in clear thinking
blisters from holding
a gun at your temple
some clarity on mysteries
a theory of shoes left by the roadside
a left shoe
triumphalism with respect to cream cake
this photograph of a spruce
more than you can take
all that remains
whomever you think will listen
you will need unhappy secrets
you will need a way out
you will need something to read
to soften
to frame
to jostle
to rebuke
something to condemn
something with waves in it
you will need distortions

and polygons
and unfair assessments
you will need a tongue phantom
an incomprehensible questionnaire
neighbors peering through window blinds
you will need cliché
pastorals
invective
compression
hieroglyphics
and, for this experiment, you will need
good intentions
dark suspicions
and the theory of a life lived
in lists
in careful negotiations
in boxes
in Möbius strips
in trouble
in fact
in case
you will need, for this experiment
everything you lost
each time you forgot
one by one
evasion
convection
you will need to ask for directions
for this experiment
to work
to yield
to transpose
to falter
to fail.
You will need it all
and, don't you know
you will need
a coat.

Watching an Algerian Crime Show
in Frankfurt, Germany,
January 26, 2018, 3 a.m. (Friday)

—For Angela Schwickert, German Composer and
　Tayeb Saddiki, French-Moroccan Dramatist

Something is wrong with the evidence
in this scene, and the actors seem to know
their characters should doubt "coincidence."

But like any story needing some place to go,
this one turns on twists and misdirection,
not least by the director himself, at pains to show

how Detective Nasser, in the act of crime detection,
sends messages by text to a shadowy Parisian,
possibly sabotaging Inspector Malik's inspection.

And they keep looking beyond the television
screen, right out of North Africa, directly at me,
but I'd rather not help them. I like the illusion

of a world where someone else solves the mystery,
where by the end of act two, I'm still clueless
enough to be surprised by the cheap flattery

from a dead giveaway or, even better, a lucky guess.
Naturally, I keep my luck to myself and pretend
I saw the solution before the killer could confess,

which is every good actor's method in the end,
but what to do then about this impossible narrative:
There's a parallel plot around the victim's missing hand,

a wedding band in Lisbon rose-gold: tasteful, expensive
proof enough for Nasser that someone once was happy,
had long walks under Iberian birches, was grateful to be alive.

Among castle ruins on the Rhine, watching TV in Germany,
I have to wonder if justice begins not with fairness, but love.
Of course, so much of this night is a stumbling memory,

lost to wild speculation, grasping for facts, and a naïve
hope that the line between two troubles is straight;
and, in any event, who knows what's left to believe?

See here a montage of Inspector Malik, alone at night,
dreaming of eating almond butter cookies with Paul Bowles,
crème au chocolat and cardamom syrup of ex-patriot wit

on the terrace of Le Continental, casting Berber spells
across an expanse of beach over the harbor lights to Spain.
Now, a platoon of Tunisian undercover cops prowls

like a rumor through Souk Ahras; I'm sure I've seen
this before. Yes, they're searching not for a hand but a ring,
any ring, that might call out in an alchemical refrain:

one found metal object reaching for a lost, a magic Sonar ping
in medieval dead reckoning, of "action over a distance"
as even Einstein thought possible. I've caught the director hoping

I can't tell the difference between plot and providence,
that I'm willing to trade something like reason for faith
in fantasies of quantum physics. In my experience,

it is possible at three in the morning: the mad truth
of logic flowing backward to the ghost inside a name,
chance operations leading from, say, the labyrinth

of a market in Marakech to a murderer, waiting for his plane
to land far from the law, some place away from death.

Ceci N'est Pas un Oiseau

Icarus wants to be explicit on this point
as one might imagine the reference unclear:
the tragic part is predictable, even quaint
given what flying is, to say nothing of the air,
and anyway, what's the harm in another lunatic
acting a fool on his own time, crazy "off the clock"
like a good citizen, even willing to let us laugh
at him because maybe laughter is proof enough
that whoever finally splashes down was pushed
up first, perhaps weeping and pale with vertigo
toward a point unobservable to those who wished
to watch it all from the ground. Maybe letting go
is not what it seems, maybe it's a science, after all
or some high art of holding on, and then the fall.

Charon's Lament

The lately dead are selfish and clever
in their refusal to accept the end.
Life is over. Nothing lasts forever.

Look at them: waiting to cross my river,
dilettantes playing at pretend;
the lately dead are selfish and clever

enough to game a system that never
fails and break rules that not even I can bend.
Life is over. Nothing lasts forever.

Some—thinking we're all in this together—
refer to me as their "eccentric friend"
just one of the family in my severe

gothic drag. Who can say whether
such effrontery is hard to defend,
given that they're as dead as their endeavor,

a truth I treasure like any believer
who longs for eternity. I recommend
to the lately dead, the selfish, the clever:
Get over your lives. Nothing lasts forever.

This is Only a Test

Critics have contended that the machine [the CERN Hadron Particle Accelerator] could produce a black hole that could eat the Earth or something equally catastrophic.

—*New York Times*

Let me see if I understand this. Just outside Geneva, in a land of neutral zones, scientists and pretenders to science are contemplating a particle collision experiment that some believe could open a black hole and end the world: cascading protons, shot in opposite directions at ninety-nine percent of the speed of light around a giant, underground, electromagnetic doughnut.

Certain things are infinite, I suppose, and others last what, a trillionth of a second(?), the length of time they are measuring in Switzerland, staging that instant after the Big Bang. And it turns out that part of the machine is actually in France, which gives me hope.

The truth is I want to trust the romance of a visionary madness, to look past the apocalyptic overtones—because that's what I do— and toward a myth, a dream of revelation, a quantum state of insight. To prepare for this, I might recall Icarus plummeting from some unimaginable height, his wings melted not so much by the heat of Apollo's flaming chariot as, rather, by the light of close scrutiny, of observable facts, or by the received view that humans should not fly. Perhaps it is a consolation to find, in those black-and-white film clips of absurdly planes flapping, gyrating, churning, twirling, some argument for the failure of any rational enterprise. And one could do worse than to wind up in a Bruegel painting, each day, dressing up for the same lyrical end, replaying, repeating, returning again, to the limits of philosophy and Flemmish high culture, that moment when it went wrong.

Like so much else, the Hadron Collider's properly working mechanism is a question of temperature regulation. One is warned never to burn bridges, either real or metaphorical. Keeping one's cool is a first principle in polite company. And it is basic to our shared experience that an overcooked egg becomes an art installation. Einstein, an American émigré, won the Nobel Prize not for his work on relativity, but for a study of the photoelectric effect, a study of light, of heat. Every time I burn my fingers changing a light-bulb, it occurs to me that—because sixty-watts of light produce seventy-seven degrees of ambient radiation, two-hundred sixty degrees of surface radiant heat, and over four-thousand at its vacuum core—illumination is morally ambiguous. Thus are we known to be ambivalent about Good and Evil but fastidious on the question of Hot and Cold.

At some point, someone, presumably, must turn the machine on, a gesture of anticipatory grace, nostrums sweeping over the altar, an entire aesthetic of desire held in flux in the circumference of a colossal zero buried under the cathedrals of ancient Europa. If we are to glimpse something numinous lost to numerical puzzles, taking up the timeline in a coil around the hand, under the elbow, the cosmological extension cord put away, then I want to see what Icarus sees in the instant just after his wings dissolve but before he falls. I want to record the discipline of sixteenth-century paint and Greek fantasy; a family of many artists, and Pieter Bruegel the Elder who signed his work with a misspelling of his own name.

At the sub-atomic level, I'm watching myself composing my signature, the lurid and unseemly continuity of letters flowing out of themselves, into the encoded space of a blank page. I see unmappable shorelines of identity looping endlessly around the alphabet, reeling through catalogs of imperfectly dotted i's, blind concessions to fate over and over without irony, the vague memory of breakfast with a stranger under a hastily scribbled sun or telephone doodles dutifully retraced, forever if necessary, until I get it right.

About the Author

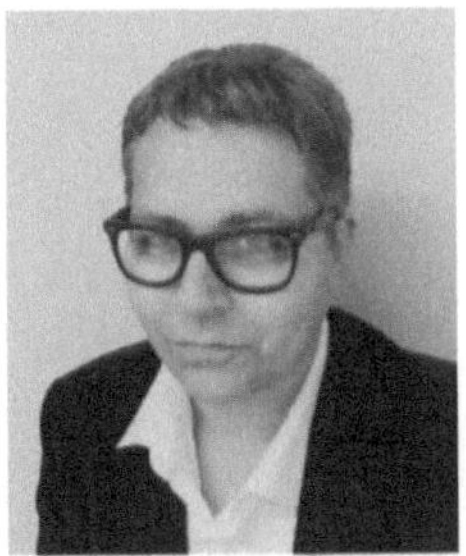

Carey Scott Wilkerson is the author of numerous plays, including *Seven Dreams of Falling, Ariadne in Exile, The Revised Diagnosis of the Minotaur's Head*, and *The Secret History of an Unseen Thing*. Additionally, he is the author of four opera libretti: *The Ariadne Songs* and *The Rescue* (with composer Angela Schwickert); *Eddie's Stone Song: Odyssey of the First Pasaquoyan* (with composer James Ogburn); and *The Heart is a Lonely Hunter* (with composer Robert Chumbley). Wilkerson is editor (with poet Melissa Dickson) of *Stone, River, Sky: An Anthology of Georgia Poems* and author of the poetry collection *Threading Stone*. His works for the stage have been produced in Los Angeles at the Lillian Theatre, The Eclectic Company Theater, and the Ivar Performance Research Group; in Oregon at the Collaborative Theatre Project; in New York at SUNY's Staller Center for the Arts; in Illinois at the Millikin University Opera Theatre; in Atlanta at the Center for Contemporary Art; in Columbus, GA at the River Center for the Performing Arts, in Buena Vista at Pasaquan, and in Germany at the Saulheim Sängerhalle, the Wiesbaden Konzertplatz, and at the Junge Opera Rhein-Main Konservatorium, Frankfurt. He is a Pushcart Prize-nominated poet, a recipient of the Columbus State University Creative Endeavors Prize, recipient of two Lillian E. Smith Writing Fellowships, and a Core Faculty member of Reinhardt University's Low-Residency MFA Creative Writing Program. He holds a Ph.D. from Georgia State University and is Assistant Professor of Creative Writing at Columbus State University.